NO MORE
CHAINS

NO MORE CHAINS

LATINA TEELE

Lita D. Ward
Editorial Midwife Publishing

Ordering Information

Quantity sales. Special discounts are available on quantity purchases by corporations, associations, and others. Orders by trade bookstores and wholesalers. Please contact Latina Teele at latinateele@gmail.com or visit her website www.latinateele.org.

Editing & Publishing

Lita P. Ward, the Editorial Midwife
LPW Editing & Consulting Services, LLC
www.litapward.com

Published in the United States of America by
Editorial Midwife Publishing

Book Cover:

Photographer: Jaylen Rodgers
Designer: BVS Images & Designs Marketing,
Advertisement & Promotions

ISBN: 9798638812980

ALSO BY LATINA TEELE

Be Loosed to Be Used

Breaking Free

Worship at The Well

Living Every Day in God's Presence

FOREWORD

Throughout the Bible of old, during crucial times in the lives of his people, God would always raise up a prophet, a preacher, a teacher, a people or one crying in the wilderness... with a word that would turn a people back to God and back to the cross! Such as God has done in the life of this anointed woman of God, Pastor/Prophet Latina Teele; for such a time as this!

In the book of Esther, Esther declared if I perish, I perish, but she had to go in obedience to God, to stand in the gap for them or they all would perish. Esther made up her mind to obey what the man of God, Mordecai had told her to do. She had to find a way and she did through fasting and prayer.

Esther knew her assignment through Mordecai her uncle; who groomed her for the Lord to use at that crucial time in the history of the Israelites. Thank God she had a mentor who heard from the Lord. You will see in the writing of this book *No More Chains*, Pastor/Prophet Teele had to obey the voice of God to pen the book and there was a set time for it to come forth. Now, after years of "Breaking Free" Conferences, she had to sit down and write.

Pastor/Prophet Teele heard the Lord in prayer asking her to "seek Me early" that I might reveal My will and My purpose unto you. She pursued God, laying on her face before Him, in fasting and in prayer. Oftentimes being led by the Holy Spirit, going weeks without food as she sought the Lord. Out of this season of birthing, God gave her Breaking Free Ministries.

When a person is not free, they are tormented with depression, oppression, fear, shame, loneliness, and all manner of demons chasing after them. It takes someone walking in power and authority to set them free. Pastor/Prophet Teele specializes in this type deliverance.

She ministers in the Spirit, through the Word of God to bring clarity to the people of God. Also, she ministers in song, until there is hardly anyone left standing, but slain in the Spirit; some in worship, or just weeping before the Lord. Pastor Teele is an anointed woman of God for this hour in the Kingdom.

In this book, you will find many nuggets of revelation, wisdom, knowledge and many examples of God revealing Himself unto Pastor/ Prophet Teele. As you read this book, may I suggest that you find a quiet place to read, because it will have you oftentimes weeping, because you can see a part of yourself being LOOSED! Other times you will be in worship.

This will be one of those books for your library. Don't miss this one; it will be a best seller! For there are many people that are in the pain of bondage for years who want to be loosed and set free by the power of God! They are seeking for someone like this woman of God who walks in the power of Holy Spirit. May the Lord bless you, as you seek Him, and while reading this book that you be LOOSED FROM THE CHAINS THAT BIND!

~ Hattie Hopkins, Sr. Pastor of Redeeming Faith International Ministries, Inc.

TABLE OF CONTENTS

ACKNOWLEDGEMENTS

I would like to first thank God for the gift He has placed upon my life. I will not take it for granted and abuse God's gift. I would like to thank my family, my husband Michael of 30 years and our children Michael, Latilya, Jeremiah and my special God-daughter NyAriyon (MiMi). I thank God for my mother for always being there. My greatest inspiration during this season of writing this book is my daughter Latilya Teele. During the times when I felt like stopping, she always gave me that last push.

I thank God for my birthing church family who keep me covered in prayer, Overseer Ronnie Staton, Pastor Angel Staton and House of Refuge Church family. I would like to thank Bishop Frederick, Pastor Hattie and Redeeming Faith International Ministries for so much love and support shown to my family and me.

INTRODUCTION

T his book, *No More Chains* was birthed from the song, "No More Chains" the moment God suddenly touched me and inspired me to write. Even more, this book is biblically inspired from the Scripture, John 8:36. *If the Son therefore shall make ye free, ye shall be free indeed.* This is one of my favorite Scriptures, which reveals to me that I can live every day free from bondage. Since Jesus has paid the price for me to be free, chains can no longer hold me captive to traditions and manmade rules. Once Jesus sets you free, you are truly free indeed. God sent his only begotten Son to die on the cross. He was crucified; therefore, Jesus was bruised just for me! God resurrected Him on the third day and that same power has set me free! Once God loose you from your chains, stay free. Galatians 5:1...*Stand fast therefore in the liberty (freedom) where with Christ hath made us free and be not entangled again with the yoke of bondage.*

Keep professing no more chains over your life and family. Don't be entangled again with bondage. There are so many people right in the church bound; bound people trying to free bound people. How can the blind lead the blind? Get yourself free so you can go strengthen your brother and sister.

In this book, you will gain keys in getting yourself free from bondage. Sometimes bondage is inherited from generational curses. If you find yourself staggered, depressed, oppressed, disobedient, lost, bitter, walking in unforgiveness, that is a sign that you are bound. Come to the knowledge and understanding of God that you need and want to be free. Allow this book to minister unto your heart and declare and decree there will be no more chains in your life!

CHAPTER 1

Come Out of the Prison!

P rison is a place or state of confinement. Whatever has you in bondage is literally your prison. If you are not at liberty to do what God has ordained you to be doing, then you are in prison! When Paul and Silas were thrown into the Roman prison at Philippi, the jailer bound their feet in stocks (Acts 16:23-24). Paul was again bound with chains in the Jerusalem Tower of Antonia in Acts 21:33-37, which his Roman citizenship freed him. That was an example of a prison in the natural, but God loosed them supernaturally, and God wants to do the same miracle for you. Chains represent bondage and it is not of God. His will is for us to be free and free indeed! The jailers may have bound Paul and Silas' feet, but they couldn't bind their hearts. Read Acts 16:25-29. Verse 25 states, *"And at midnight Paul and Silas prayed and sang praises unto God..."* People will try to literally put chains on you, but God will keep your heart! God will even keep your mind and soul stayed on Him. Paul and Silas could have become discouraged or depressed, but instead they began to sing praises to God. Same as today, when it feels like chains have you yoked up, begin to sing and praise God. Watch those chains begin to drop off! I've seen God do this a countless number of times. I was so heartbroken and bound, but God! I would begin to walk through my house and praise God. Within a few minutes, I would feel those chains breaking off.

Let's get back to the story about Paul and Silas in prison. These guys were thrown into prison for calling a devil out of a girl. This is the same as today as I have personally experienced. I was placed in a box because I was delivering too many people. I recall someone inviting me to their church and the person was rebuked by their pastor for inviting a deliverance preacher to their church, who was me! After I got the word of her being rebuked, I still kept right on casting out demons, setting the captives free. And, I kept right on singing praises unto God. Paul and Silas were imprisoned because of their operating in their gifts. Sadly, even now, people are being trapped in a box only because they desire to obey God in operating their God-given gifts. Though I was once there, I praise God because He has set me free from prison; no more chains holding me.

Paul and Silas were cast into prison for calling unclean spirits out of a damsel. This girl was a fortune teller and when Paul casted the unclean spirits from her, her masters became angry (Acts 16:16). Even though they were thrown into a physical prison with their feet fastened with chains, those chains were not able to hold Paul and Silas bound. They had God working for them.

I don't know who or what is trying to hold you bound with chains, but believe me, they will not hold you if you put your trust in God and lean not to your own understanding. Those chains will fall off of you! Paul and Silas kept a positive mindset in a bad situation. This is what you must do as well. Keep yourself grounded in God. I promise you those chains won't be able to hold you down. Believe God at His Word that He has set you free indeed. Get a song in your heart and praise on your lips and watch God. The Bible says, "At midnight Paul and Silas prayed, and sang praises to God. Suddenly, there was a great earthquake, so that the foundation of the prison was shaken. Immediately all the doors were opened and everyone bands were loosed" (Acts 16:25-26). God came in and broke those chains off both of them.

I don't care how strong the chains on your life have you bound, it's not a match to our matchless God! Every chain is going to break loose off you. There was too much work for God to do in Paul and Silas to remain in prison bound. Well, it is the same for you! There is too much work in you to be bound in prison. When I was bound in prison, I could not worship, write books, write and record songs, or do women conferences. I was stagnated and stuck in one frame of mind. Nothing was happening in my life, but when I allowed God to come into my heart and break the chains off of me, things began to happen. I am free to worship, write, and do what God has called me to do. What a wonderful feeling to be free with no more chains!

While in that prison, I was held captive in my mind and heart. My soul was even locked up. My God! However, I opened my heart and let God have His way! I said, "Lord, no more chains. I just can't do this any longer. I want to be free in You; not just going through the motions of church."

It was a form of godliness but denying the power of God. That power is that God sent his only begotten Son to die on the cross, raised Him from the dead on the third day and set me free. Until we really accept that in our heart and believe, we will be bound by traditions, and man-made rules. God holds your future and has purpose for your life. Yes, even you in church going through the motions. There is more for you than those four walls! Set yourself free, loose the chains and be about your Father's business. Declare and decree there will be no more chains!

CHAPTER 2

Chains on Your Gifts

I s it possible that we could be operating in gifts, yet bound with chains? Yes, I believe it! I am a witness that you can be operating in your gift God gave you, but at the same time bound. Roman's 11:29 says, "For the gifts and calling of God are without repentance." God will not take back His gifts He has given us. Once God gives us a gift, it is ours. If we don't use the gift for the glory of God, it's like having chains on your gift. Does your gift have heavy weights on it holding it bound?

I remember being in church with gifts that I knew God had given me, but I allowed the opinions of people to put chains on my gifts. The gifts laid dormant and stagnated. I was all tied up and tangled up in chains with a gift to sing, teach, and prophesy! Sometimes it felt like my tongue was glued to the top of my mouth from fear. One of the greatest chains that bound my gifts was fear! I feared being judged by the church. I feared even myself of messing up and being embarrassed. So, as I write I can be honest and let you know, yes you can have gifts with chains on them.

Another chain is intimidation. Sometimes you can allow other people's gifts to intimidate you. God made us all differently and no one's gifts are identical. We are all made in the likeness of God in a unique way. He gave all of us gifts to use for His glory, and it's no place in the church or anywhere else to be intimated by someone else's gift.

Maybe you can't sing like Yolanda Adams, but whatever gift of singing God has given you, just use it for His glory. Everyone with the gift of singing will not go to the televised Gospel Celebration or win a Grammy. Maybe your gift of singing is to edify the church or body of Christ. Or your gift of singing is to usher people into God's presence! Don't put chains on your gift just because God didn't give it to you like someone's else gift. I am guilty of that. I am a worshipper and love singing worship songs to God's glory. I love ushering people into God's presence, and it makes me happy. Once upon a time, I thought my gift of singing was for another grand platform, but no, it is just for what God called it to be, and that is for Him to be glorified in song and to usher people into His presence. The chains are now off my gift of singing and I'm so grateful. Take the chains off your gift and use it for God!

Another way chains can be on your gift is when you're trying to operate in a gift, and you know you are in sin! As I said earlier, gifts are without repentance, meaning just because you begin to indulge in sinful actions, it does not mean God will take the gift from you. However, God's anointing and glory will be lifted off of it. There are many people walking in their gifts with no anointing on the gift. This is what I call chains on their gift. They're entangled and all tied up in sin, but continue to sing, teach, preach, usher, or whatever their gift is. Nevertheless, they will continue in it with chains. An evangelist can come from out of town where no one in town really knows them except the person who invited them. That evangelist can be entangled in fornication, pornography, lust, lies and all sorts of sin; but still have a gift of exhortation. I mean can really hype the crowd and excite them. The church will be up in a praise on high, because that evangelist operates in their gift. What will be missing though is the anointing and glory of God! Even God said He'll make room for the gift, but where is the anointing? It is the anointing that makes the difference and destroys the yoke!

You may have a hyped crowd, but were any blinded eyes opened, any lame walked, or did someone get delivered with the evidence of purging out? Better yet, were any yokes destroyed in the service? The latter part of Isaiah 10:27 clearly says, "The yoke shall be destroyed because of the anointing. Yes, a few yokes may have been broken, but were they destroyed at the root? If not, then that is a sign that some chains are operating within your gift.

I love how God is not an Indian giver, as we say. God does not operate like man. Man will give you something, but if you mess up, they may ask for the gift back. God will allow you to keep the gift, but once you step out of His will, He will allow you to keep going with no anointing. The people will sit at conferences and tent revivals deceived and manipulated by people operating with chains on their gifts because many do not have the gift of the discernment. God has given me the discernment of spirits so as I sit in services and listen to the preacher, singer or teacher scream all they want, I sit there and discern that it is not of God! They have chains on their gifts. I call it "hiding behind your gift"; however, you cannot hide from God and you cannot hide from God's people with the discernment of spirits. That is a gift we all need, so we can stop being deceived by false prophets. There are many preachers with chains in their preaching, full of pride, arrogance and high-mindedness. If you are always talking about how great your anointing is that is a sign you are tied and tangled up with chains. If you are always bragging on yourself, you are tied up with chains on your gift. The sad part is no one can tell us anything. Check your gift to be sure you do not have chains on your gift.

CHAPTER 3

Chains are Yokes!

A yoke is a heavy, wooden harness that fits over the shoulders of an ox or oxen. It is attached to a piece of equipment the oxen are to pull. You carrying a yoke around your neck is like carrying chains around your neck. Yokes are a form of bondage just as chains are bondage. Anything holding you from moving is bondage. This is why Jesus said to take my yoke upon you, and learn of me, for I am meek and lowly in heart; and ye shall find rest unto your souls (Matthew 11:29). Unless we take the yoke of God, we will be in bondage under any other kind of yoke.

Jesus said, "My yoke is easy and my burden is light." This Scripture alone informs us that man's yoke, and the cares of this world's yoke are burdensome. The world's yoke will depress and oppress you. However, Jesus promised to give us rest. I stress getting free, loosening the chains and yokes from your life, because that is a terrible life to live. I remember having yokes around my neck to the point I became depressed. I had allowed people and circumstances to put a yoke around my neck. It is the unhappiest life to live. When yokes are around your neck, we will try to dress it up, make it up, and even act like everything is okay. We will walk around like it is normal to live in bondage. Sometimes you can live in bondage for so long that it becomes normal. After a time, you won't even know you have yokes around your neck. Many of you are bound and trapped and don't even realize it. The yoke has been around your neck so long that it feels normal and it is time to loose the yoke from around your neck and get moving. Isaiah 82:2 says, "Shake thyself from the dust; arise, and sit down, O Jerusalem: loose thyself from the bands of thy neck, O captive daughter of Zion." God is saying it is time to arise and shake loose! It's time to loose the yoke from your neck. You have been captive long enough; shake the devil loose and free yourself from bondage!

Yokes are strongholds. Isaiah 58:6 says, "Is not this the fast that I have chosen? To loose the bands of wickedness to undo the heavy burdens, and to let the oppressed go free, and that ye break every yoke?" God's Word plainly states some devils, strongholds, and wickedness are not leaving or coming down until we fast! God wants every yoke broken off of your life. If you have been battling for years with this yoke of bondage, this means only one thing...it is time to declare a real fast and break this yoke off your neck. Call a fast to undo the heavy burdens. Jesus said to cast all of your burdens on Him, so why are you trying to carry them? I'm dealing with some yokes in my family right now as I write this book. Only three days ago, I declared a fast. I got up that day and said, "Enough is enough devil! You will not continue to mess with my children. This yoke will be broken in Jesus' name. Every chain of bondage will be destroyed by the power of God!" I declared a fast according to God's Word. I'm determined to beak every yoke of bondage and lose all bands of wickedness. I asked you to do the same thing as well. Stop allowing the enemy to put yokes on your family. God gave you your family, so fight like never. Fasting prepares us for the battle. Remember, Joshua would tell the children of Israel to prepare for battle, to fast! This what I do regularly in my life to keep me focus on God. I always fast to protect the anointing on my life. It's the anointing that is going break the yoke of bondage.

Isaiah 10:27: "And it shall come to pass in that day, that his burden shall be taken away from off thy shoulder, and his yoke from off thy neck, and the yoke shall be destroyed because of the anointing."

So, why play around with the anointing on your life? A gift will not destroy the yoke. As I said earlier in the book, gifts are without repentance. You can keep praying, singing, preaching, or teaching with a gift, but no anointing. When you come up against a strong yoke of bondage, it is not going to break and be destroyed until the anointing comes. People can continue to play church, but you will not have the anointing with your playing. Devils will not tremble at your playing church; therefore, begin to walk holy

25

before God, fast and pray, and present your life unto God. Protect that anointing and watch some walls begin to come tumbling down because the anointing destroys the yoke. Whatever you are facing in your life, whether it is yokes on your children, finances, health, and ministry, trust God and walk in faith, walk in the anointing of God. Fast and pray and watch God loose the yoke off your neck so you can run your race in the fullness. Chains are yokes and the anointing will destroy them!

CHAPTER 4

You Have the Keys to Unlock the Chains!

O n some chains there is a lock attached to it; therefore, you will need a key to unlock the lock to loose the chains. Or you will need the key to chain up what needs to be chained or secured. God has given us the keys to loose and bind. Why are we not using our keys? Is it because we do not know we have the keys to loose the chains of bondage, or bind the works of evil? "Verily I say unto you, whatsoever ye shall bind on earth shall be bound in heaven: and whatsoever ye shall loose on earth shall be loosed in heaven" (Matthew 18:18). God was telling Peter, "I have given you the authority to lose and bind because I have given you the keys. Why are you walking around with chains on you when the authority is on the inside of you?"

It is sad to say, but many Christians are walking around defected and yet, they do not have to be. The power lies down on the inside of us. Many just don't read the Word of God nor believe God at His Word. You must know this authority is in you to use it. Same as if you had keys to a door and you didn't know you had the key. Well, you would sit there until someone brought you the keys to unlock the door. If you knew you had the keys already, why would you stand on the outside waiting to go in? It is the same in the spiritual realm. Since you have the keys to bind up the bands of the enemy, use them! You have the keys to loose what belongs to you, now use them! Use your keys and declare no more chains! There is a lock on your heart to love again, because you have been hurt so many times. You are wondering, "Can I ever love again?" Unlock that chain on your heart because you can love again. However, it is going to start with you forgiving everyone who has hurt you in the past. Let them go and forgive them so you can love again. Maybe that husband abused you mentally and physically, but that does not mean the next man that comes into your life, will abuse you. If you are still holding that in your heart, then when the person God sends to you comes, you will reject him or her. Loose that hurt and unforgiveness; be healed and move forward. Declare, "No more chains!"

I've seen this happen so many times, even with myself. My first boyfriend really hurt me, and when my husband came along, I was fearful of getting into a serious relationship. I was still hurting and had unforgiveness buried deep within. I could have missed out on a good husband because of the chains that were in my heart. I felt like I couldn't love again, and God loosened my heart. I found love again. My husband and I have been married for 28 years. Healing had to take place first; I had to bind and lock up all of those memories of hurt and move forward. We have the power to release what belongs to us. Love belongs to the children of God. Don't allow how people who once treated you or hurt you in the past cause you to walk in bitterness. A bitter heart will not allow even the sweetest person in. Let the healing begin in your heart. Use your keys and loose that love back into your heart. Loose the unforgiveness in your heart. I thank God I found love again and was able move forward instead of backwards in my life. I thank God I love those that have mistreated me in the past. Those chains are off me, and no longer holding me bound.

God wants to do the same for you. I know they hurt you and even used you, but we must do as the bible says to love those that despitefully use you. Use your key to lock and bind up that bitterness. If you don't, you are going to treat people the way you have been treated in the past. Hurting people hurt people. It is a cycle, repeating itself. Don't sow the same bad seeds that were sown into your life. My husband has asked me many times how can I be so forgiving of others. He has witnessed people hurting me, using me, and falsely accusing me. "Do what?" I asked.

"Love and bless people that you know have hurt you, used you, judged you and even despised you," he responded.

I told my husband, "It is the love of God. I refuse to give the devil victory over my life."

God has given me the keys to loose and bind, so I'm just using my keys when you see me love those that hate me! I have the power on the inside of me to bind up that bitterness and hatred when it comes to tempt me. Yes, I have thoughts of "you don't need to bless them. Don't you remember what they said or did to you?" God has given us the power to resist those negative thoughts, and yield to His loving spirit. Those are our keys, but many are not using their keys. Some are allowing people to bring them into bondage. Everyone who holds unforgiveness, causes a chain to attach to their heart. The power is in us and the keys are in our hands, but we are not using what God has already given us. God said, "He's able to do exceedily, abundantly above all we can ask or think!" (Ephesians 3:20) Get this...*according to the power that works in us*! That means we have the power within. God will do great things in our lives when we activate the power on the inside of us. God is in control but there is some work for us to do as well. You have the power to loose the chains off your life, so use your keys!

CHAPTER 5

The Spirit of Herod and Pharaoh

The Spirit of Herod

You may be asking yourself, *what is the spirit of Herod and Pharaoh?* Well, you are about to find out. In these last days, God is about to expose the spirit of Herod and Pharaoh which is operating in pastors and leaders. Herod is a name of several Roman rulers in the Palestine region during Jesus' earthly ministry and the periods shortly before His birth and after His resurrection. There was Herod the Great, which was the eldest son of Antipater. Herod the Greek established his authority and influence through well-built fortresses, and foreign solders. To assure his continued rule, he slaughtered all male infants who could possibly be considered legal heirs to the throne. There were also Herod Archelaus, who was the son of Herod the Great. Archelaus (a name meaning "leading the people") came to power after the death of his father Herod the Great. All of them were in control of the land when they took their place on the throne.

Jesus was born in Bethlehem during the reign of Herod the Great. When the wise men asked where this child, King of the Jews was born, it caused Herod to become suspicious and jealous. According to Matthew 2, Herod ordered for all male infants to be slaughtered because he was threatened by Jesus. Same as it is today, there is a spirit rising in leaders, and that spirit is jealousy and intimidation. I know it is sad to think this way or even to believe it, but it is true. Some leaders are beginning to act like God, and God is not pleased. He did not place the people under leadership to be lord over or controlled by them. Leaders must lead, not lord. I have seen leaders walk in the Spirit of Herod when they have a young minister under them. If that young minister is extremely anointed, the pastor will become intimidated and may try to silence the young minister. That is a spirit of Herod in operation. If God has anointed you with gifts and you are unable to operate in those gifts because your leader will not release you to do so, this is bondage. It is the spirit of Herod to kill the gift within you. I advise you to flee like Joseph did with Baby Jesus. Matthew 2:14-15 says, "When he arose, he took the young child and his mother by night and departed into Egypt and was there until the death of Herod." Joseph had to take Baby Jesus and run for his life. That is how powerful Jesus was and is! He had to go into hiding as an infant, because his enemy was trying to track him down to destroy His mission. God warned the wise men not to lead Herod to Jesus. Even today, God is going to warn His children when the spirit of Herod is trying to hunt them down to destroy the anointing on their lives. Herod wanted to keep control of the throne, and he did all he could to destroy Jesus, not knowing God had a greater throne for His only begotten Son.

A leader may be trying to silence you because they are intimidated by your drawing people to God and gaining popularity in the city. Not knowing that the call on your life is so much greater than a city; God has called you to the nations! In reality, your main focus is saving souls, setting the captive free, and moving in the Spirit of God. Sometimes because you are focused on souls, you are mistaken to just be trying to gain a crowd, when all the time, you are more so preparing yourself for the nations! The Spirit of Herod knows this so he tries to kill your spirit before you can even get out of the city. Do like Joseph and hide yourself from the enemy. Joseph didn't try to fight back; he just listened to God, fled and hid the Baby Jesus. Stay connected in the Spirit of God; He will lead and guide you to the finish line. Jesus' finish line was the cross, 30 long years, but He completed His mission. If you are under leadership and you know the Spirit of Herod is in operation over your life, I advise you to stay at the feet of Jesus. Be still and quiet, until God gives you a way of escape. When God does, run for your life. Don't allow anybody and anything to destroy what God has placed in your life.

The Spirit of Pharaoh

Pharaoh was the title of the Kings of Egypt. In the Egyptian language, the word *Pharaoh* means "Great House, his honor, his majesty." Pharaoh held the children of Israel in bondage, until God sent His deliverer to lead the people out of bondage, and that deliverer was known as Moses!

The Spirit of Pharaoh is another spirit that controls the people of God prohibiting them from operating in their God-given gifts. Pharaoh literally bound the people with chains, but God sent Moses to set the captives free, using him to lead the children of Israel through the Red Sea. In Exodus 1:9-12, Pharaoh said, "The people of Israel are mightier than us; come let us deal wisely with them lest they multiply." Therefore, they set over them two masters to afflict the children of Israel with burdens but the more they afflicted them, the more they would multiply. God promised the children of Israel would suffer many afflictions, but He would deliver them from them all. The more Pharaoh tried to bind up and torment the children of Israel, the more God made a way of escape. He tried to destroy them, but each time God delivered His children. Pharaoh had enslaved the people of God to the point many were bound unto death. This is a spirit of control and has gone on a rampage in the church. Many leaders are walking in the Spirit of Pharaoh and their people are sitting under them bound in their minds. God has not set a woman or man over a flock of people to keep them in bondage. Jesus came to set the captives free.

If you are a leader and all you do is control the people, this is not of God. If you are beating them down every Sunday and fussing from the pulpit, this is bondage. God sent grace and mercy and that Grace is Jesus Christ! It is bondage when you make your flock feel like they have sinned because they have missed a Sunday from church. That is not the loving spirit of our Father. If you're condemning your people, this is not God. He said He came to save the world and not to condemn the world. A Pharaoh spirit will keep chains on you to the point you will become complacent, stagnated, and spiritually dead; just going through the motions of church. That Pharaoh spirit does not want you to grow. It will only allow you to go so far and then it will snatch you back, if it looks like you are about to conquer something in your life.

Read Exodus 1. Every time the children of Israel would multiply, this was a sign of growth. Pharaoh would tell the slave masters to make their burdens heavier. This was set up to eventually kill them. Pharaoh began to fear the children of Israel, to the point he told the Hebrew midwives to kill every male child that the Hebrew women would birth. However, this was the only control Pharaoh had. He ordered every male child to be tossed into the river. But God always intervenes. Even with Moses, God had someone there to rescue him because he had a mission to complete. That mission was to deliver the children of Israel from the hands of Pharaoh! God loosed them from the chain of bondage.

Control is a dangerous form of bondage. God is about to free His people from leaders holding people down in bondage, just because they are jealous and intimidated by gifts and callings in a person's life. I declare and decree no more chains on your life! I pray God reveals to you where this spirit is coming from and that He will give you the power to loose yourself from these chains. If you are under leadership and you know you are called and gifted, God has also made your leader aware of what is in you. If this is you and you are not walking out your calling, this is bondage. God want you under a spiritual father or mother who will nourish that gift, not pacify it to keep it under bondage. He wants you under leadership that will chastise you, but at the same time love you and train you up to be a great leader. He will not smother or bury your gift. This is a spirit of Pharaoh to kill what is in you. But you must take a stand. Do not disrespect leadership, but go before God and ask God to show you how to release yourself from that ministry. This is with the intent to grow and become all God has ordained you to be. You must declare and decree no more chains in your own life. Loose yourself from the Spirits of Herod and Pharaoh!

CHAPTER 6

Stagnated

C hains keep you from moving! Do you feel sometimes like you are in a stand-still mode in your life? Do you feel like you are just not moving? If you feel this way, it is because you are stagnated. Stagnated means to be still, or settled, not moving. Some of you are not moving and it is a possibility that you have chains on you. Chain means to fasten, bind or tie down. Chains will cause you to be in one place. Some of you have been in the same place for years. Years with a calling and gifting on your life, but you're stuck! You're stagnated and not moving in the direction God has called you to. It's time to break free and walk in your liberty. God does not want you stagnated because He is a moving God. Remember, Jesus never stayed in one place. He was always moving from place to place, performing miracles. There was nothing stagnated about Jesus.

When water stands still, mosquitoes and bugs will settle in the water. Stagnated water stinks and is not good for consumption. It can make you sick. But flowing, moving, clean water is life. Out of your belly shall flow rivers of living water

(John 7:38). You must make up your mind, stir up the gifts and work out what God has placed in you. You have the power on the inside to declare no more chains! Ephesians 3:20 says, "Now unto him that is able to do exceedingly, abundantly, above all you can ask or think according to the power that's working in you." The power is in you! God has already given us what we need to be set free and we have to do the work. The power is in us to prophesy to our own selves of who we are.

I have been stuck in my life in the past. I allowed people to keep me stagnated, but it was not their fault, but mine. If you are operating on the same level after 10 years, then you are stuck. It is time to discover who you really are and God's plan for your life. I was just sitting there in church one day, witnessing to the preached Word and I said, "Go ahead, Pastor!"

Then, I heard God say, "Well, when are you going to go ahead?"

I looked around because it sounds like He was right in my ear saying it. I couldn't believe it! God pushed me right out of those chains. I started running for life. My mind was free and there were no more chains holding me! I hate the word "stagnated." Even as slow as a turtle is, he knows he has to keep moving. Because he does move slowly across the road, often times, it gets run over. It is the same with us. If we keep moving slowly than other people, they are going to run us over. The fire I have now on the inside, I actually had it 20 years ago. However,

38

during my trials and testing of my faith, I lost some fire. I almost gave up, but I had just enough fire left to stir up and rekindle. God wants you to stir up what you have left. It is not too late for Him to use you as a masterpiece for His glory. I know you have been hurt, trampled over, misunderstood, lied on, or thrown away for dead, but now is the time to stir that fire back up. I can relate to what you're going through. I have been there and almost lost all but God! Depression and oppression almost took me out because of so much hurt and disappointment.

You are too close to give up now. You may have been stuck and stagnated in one place; confined to one level, but now it is time to loose the chains of bondage and free yourself! Nobody can do this for you; this has to be your choice. Either you will stay stuck and die or get up and start living again. Many days I didn't feel like living anymore, but God freed my mind of depression and stagnated heart. I'm living my life to the fullest. No more chains! Whenever I feel like someone is trying to bring me into bondage, I will get far from them. Once you have been in prison and those chains been loosed, you never want to be in bondage again. I cannot understand people who go to prison and get freed, and they go back and do the same crazy thing that got them locked up in the first place. Maybe it is because while in jail, they really did not accept that they were in bondage. They may have said, "This is just life." It is the same as today, with people being bound so long that they believe it is just the way it is supposed to be. That is the lie the devil tells us. You can become comfortable being stagnated, stuck, and bound that you are accustomed to it. It becomes a way of life for you. This is the reason it is not good to get complacent. Once it really settles in your mind, it will trickle down to your heart. You cannot believe that it is okay to get to this state. No, it is not! Absolutely not! God has greater for you, so get yourself free. Get out of that place of confinement. Make up your mind that you will not allow people to continue to bring you under the yoke of bondage. Romans 8:15- 16 says, "For you did not receive the spirit of bondage again to fear but you received the spirit of adoption by whom we cry out, "Abba, Father." You don't have to be bound and stagnated; it is not the will of God. The power is in you to declare, "No more chains!"

CHAPTER 7

Prayer will Loose the Chains!

I f we only knew the power of prayer… I believe God is calling the people of God back to the horns of the altar. Prayer is all I know in my life right now. How can we make it without prayer? God said man ought to always pray and not to faint (Luke 18:1). If you want to see chains begin to fall, start praying. I've learned in this millennium that people will not take time to pray. Life is so busy nowadays that we neglect prayer time. I am reminded how Peter was bound in jail of no fault of his own. Peter was preaching the gospel boldly drawing souls to Christ and this made King Herod angry. Herod ordered Peter to be put into jail only to please the Jews. He delivered Peter to four quaternions of soldiers, according to the Bible. "Peter was kept in prison, but prayer was made without ceasing of the church unto God for him" (Acts 12:5). The Bible says, "Peter was sleeping between two soldiers, bound with two chains and also the keepers before the door kept the prisoners" (Acts 12:6). They had double bondage upon Peter! But they didn't know that though they had chains on Peter and had him under lock and key, he had a prayer team praying for him without ceasing! As they were praying,

Peter was being released by the power of God. "And, behold, the angel of the Lord came upon him, and a light shined in the prison: and the angel smote Peter on the side and raised him up, saying, "Arise quickly. And his chains fell from his hands" (Acts 12:7).

Those chains had to fall off Peter because people were interceding on his behalf. I don't care how bad the enemy has your love one or friend bound with chains, do not cease your prayers. I heard one preacher say, "Pray one time and leave it alone." I believe I will do like the Bible says, "Pray without ceasing." I'm not saying I will be in prayer all day. I'm saying I will continually lift my love ones up in prayer, always interceding. That's praying without ceasing. I'm not praying for my children one time and I know the devil has chains on them. No, I will pray continually for my child. Pray until something changes.

When Peter got to the door, a girl named Rhoda came to the door to answer as Peter stood knocking. She was so shocked she ran *from* the door. She couldn't believe that what they were praying for was at the door! Even the prayer team praying for Peter could not believe what they were praying for was already at the door. When Rhoda told them Peter was at the door, they told her she was crazy. You see God can answer some prayers so quickly it will make us think we're crazy. The Bible said when the prayer warriors opened the door, they were astonished. I could imagine them in that living room calling down fire! "God release Peter! Lord, loose him from the shackles of bondage; loose every chain off Peter right now God! We decree and declare Peter to be set free by the power of God!" However, when the answer (Peter) showed up at the door, they were astonished and probably in disbelief that God had already answered their prayers! So, I say to you. Keep believing God, keep praying until the answer comes to your door! Don't be surprised when God sends you your answer before you can end your prayer as the example we see here with Peter.

There is power in prayer like none other. I believe this is why the enemy fights us to not pray. He knows that God has already given us the keys to heaven and that the power lives down within us. Chains will begin to fall off as we begin to pray in the heavenly realm; praying with faith that it is already done, in Jesus' name. The situation with Peter looked hopeless. He was bound with chains and had soldiers standing on guard at his cell, but God! Nothing can hold you bound when God steps in. Those chains had to be loosed once God entered that cell. God even put the two soldiers who were guarding the door to sleep. When the soldiers woke up, Peter was gone! This is just the power of prayer.

Another powerful incident in prayer loosening chains is Paul and Silas. Paul was cast into prison for calling an uncleaned spirit out of a damsel. This girl was a fortune teller and when Paul cast an uncleaned spirit from her, it caused the masters to become furious. The Bible notes in Acts 16:23-26: "They cast Paul and Silas in prison after they had beaten them badly. They fastened their feet with chains but at midnight Paul and Silas prayed and sang praises to God. Suddenly, there was a great earthquake so that the foundation of the prison was shaken. Immediately all the doors and everyone's bands were loosed. The chains came falling off Paul and Silas and everyone around them because prayers went up! When Paul and Silas released prayer and praise to God, the doors were opened and the chains could not hold them bound any longer." I don't care what kind of chains you have, but just begin to pray and praise God and He will loose the chains of bondage. I know you may feel like the prison walls are closing in on you, but God has a plan and that plan is for you to pray until the chains fall off!

CHAPTER 8

God Can Free You From Addictions!

I don't care what kind of addictions you are struggling with; it is not too hard for God! Whether it is alcohol, drugs, or over-the-counter prescription medication, God is able to free you from that addiction. However, we first must admit we have an addiction. Years ago, I suffered with severe back pain. In 1998, my husband and our children were riding along the road. I remember this like yesterday because the enemy was trying to kill my entire family. My husband was driving, and our two children were in the backseat. Our youngest child had climbed out of her booster seat, but God allowed me to see her. My son Michael helped Latilya get back in her seat and about four minutes after he did, a truck hit us! Our car spun around and then flipped over landing upside down in a ditch. That could have been a great tragedy, but God! We walked away from that accident with not one broken bone in any of us. Nevertheless, I suffered from back pain, and this started my journey with prescription drugs. I remember experiencing so much pain in my body that my mind began to have suicidal thoughts. Many nights I was so depressed that I couldn't lift my head from my pillow.

I started on three different medications, hurting all over my body, but severely in my back. My doctor prescribed sleeping pills because I was only sleeping about three – four hours a night. Some days it felt like my body was shutting down. I remember my children running from me because when I took the medication, I hallucinated. I was really getting high from the medication. By the end of my workday, I would be anxious; ready to shower and take my medication that made me feel so good. This is how I know that people who are addicted or doing it is only because of the temporary feel good experience.

I took mine for pain and to sleep away my depression. My depression came in when I felt sorry for myself. I would hurt so much that I felt helpless. There were some days I didn't feel like a very good mother, especially when my children would see me after I took my medication. Also, I would have to make sure my husband Michael was home to care for them. The medication would put me under for about seven hours straight. In those seven hours, I heard nothing, felt nothing, and saw nothing. This was scary and not the kind of life I wanted to live. Addiction is a stronghold. There are so many people who are addicted to over-the-counter drugs and it is no different from being addicted to street drugs. It is something that has us bound to be dependent on it. Therefore, it is an addiction.

Because of the pain and depression, I found myself staying in the house more than ever. I was depressed and didn't even realize it was depression. I knew I wanted more of God, but the pain drove me to being angry and sad. I never lost my faith in God, but I did lose faith in people who couldn't recognize the cry from within. Yes, I was a godly woman; yet with a great affliction. I was misunderstood a lot because of the pain I suffered. People didn't know my pain, therefore I do not hold anything against them for not seeing me for who I was. I isolated myself a lot in those days and just wanted to study my bible and pray. I learned how to worship through my pain. Yes, the addiction was there, but I still worshipped. I was under God's grace and mercy and I knew God would deliver me!

Addiction is our flesh craving for something we shouldn't have. My flesh was saying, "You need this to go to sleep." However, I had to trust God. Sometimes, I just endured the pain. God is so good though! When you can worship God through pain and suffering, that's a mighty God. I began to wrap my life around God's presence. Every single day, I leaned on God and gave Him my pain. The pain I suffered made me want to go to sleep. Consequently, the pills were the source that gave me my peace, and not the peace the bible talks about in Philippians 4:7... "And the peace of God, which passeth all understanding, shall keep your hearts and minds through Christ Jesus." The peace from the sleeping pills were a temporary peace. Nonetheless, God's peace is everlasting. I surrendered all and just got a made-up mind. I didn't want to be on the medication any longer. It took a while to get delivered and I couldn't go to sleep for night after night. I had to trust God. I listened to worship music, laid there, and prayed. After a while of waiting on God, He began to rock me to sleep. The peace of God overtook my life. My trial of addiction to the medicine just drew me closer to God. It really was meant for evil, but God turned it around for my good! The sleeping pills actually was causing depression to settle in. However, God came in and sabotaged the devil! There were people that He wanted to be delivered through my life. So, God had to set me free! Now that I'm free, I can help someone else be loosed and set free by the power of God!

CHAPTER 9

Now That You're Free, Live!

I choose to live! "Live" is defined as conducting one's life; having positive qualities, as of warmth, vigor, vitality, brightness, brilliance; or remain in human memory or record. It's time to live. After God delivered me from those prescription drugs, I chose to move forward and live my life. The chains had me so tied down, I just did not know how to live. The pills were the chains that had me locked down. Yours may not be prescription drugs, but you know within what it is that has chains on your life, to the point you cannot live fully for Jesus.

You have to denounce that chain that has you bound and speak what Psalm 118:17 says, "I shall not die, but live, and declare the works of the Lord." God has some work for you to do! I had to realize myself that I could not die with unfinished work. I had to get a made-up mind to live and not die! God spoke to me and said, "I'm not done with you, so you might as well get up out of this death bed and live!" Glory to God! I broke loose from those chains of bondage. I'm still loosed, living my life for God in the fullness!

I love Luke 19:32. In this passage of Scripture, Jesus told His disciples to tell the owners of the donkey to loose him because He had need of it. I hear people say, "God don't need me."

I always reply, "Yes, He does! If He had need of a donkey, surely He has need of you!"

This is why God wants you free. He wants you free to live your life to the fullness so that He can use you in the fullness. If you're bound with chains, you cannot live to God's fullness. I know the enemy is telling you that there is no more life in you; he is a liar. You will live! I encourage you to get up from where you are and live! Declare Psalm 118:17 every single day of your life that you will live and not die. There is too much God has in store for your life. Many Christians today are just like I was. I was in church every Sunday, but I was spiritually dead with no life in me. I was just going through the motions of church. I was actually denying God's power to set me free like 2 Timothy states... "Having a form of godliness, but denying the power thereof." Singing in the choir or praise team, attending church duties, but at same time disobedient to callings. If God is calling us in ministry but we are just ignoring the call, going to church will not make up for our disobedience. Disobedience is disobedience. There is no half obeying God. Remember the Scriptures when God gave Saul simple instructions. He failed to fulfill all instructions to the fullness and disobeyed God. Saul didn't have to disobey God, yet he deliberately disobeyed God. God said to destroy the Amalekites and their possessions and not have any pity. However, Saul allowed King Agag to live and spared the best sheep and cattle. This was plain disobedience. Whatever God is asking you to do, obey Him and live your life to the fullest. I believe the greatest life lived is in obeying God. The most peaceful life is in obeying God. I can sense when I'm not obeying God. I feel frustrated and aggravated. You will know when God has His hands on your life, and He has asked you to do a specific assignment and you have not yielded to that assignment. There is a part of you that will be restless, disturbed in your spirit. We know when we are walking in disobedience. The thing about obeying God is, that you may have to forsake a lot and many people to walk in the obedience. This has been my life; to obey God and just live!

Once God frees you, do all you know to stay free from bondage. "Stand fast therefore in the liberty wherewith Christ has made us free, and be not entangled again with the yoke of bondage" (Galatians 5:1). I cannot stress this enough. Do not get yoked up after God frees you! Live your life free in God. People are so quick to bring you back into the bondage if you're not careful. They will remind you of your past failures and sin. Don't allow yourself to be entangled in those bondages. Run like crazy when someone comes in your life and tries to bring up your past. Tell them you don't know what they are talking about because you do not know that person anymore. They're dead and been dead a long time ago and you do not want to resurrect your past! Don't be entangled, my friend. Once God breaks you free, stay free in God! Live a peaceful, and prosperous life. This is the type of life God has ordained for you. Walk in God's love and obedience unto Him. Leave your past in the past and look towards your destiny. Live to live again with Christ Jesus, our Savior.

CHAPTER 10

Imagine This...

Imagine this... you free to live every day in God's presence! Imagine every hurt, rejection, disappointment and bondage gone from your life. Imagine yourself walking in your purpose. Imagine every chain broken off your life; every generational curse loosed off your life. I want you to take a seat and sit down and imagine yourself where God wants you. Get yourself free from any distractions, sit down and imagine you free just like God wants you. Free indeed! Imagine being who God ordained you to be. Not what man thinks you should be, but being all God has already planned for you to be.

Webster's dictionary described "imagination" as the art or power of forming a mental image of something present (evidence of things not seen) to the senses of not previously known or experienced. Get a mental picture of your destiny. Every book I ever written, I saw it mentally in my mind. I thought of it and it came into fruition. It became a reality in my life. It also starts with your faith. Hebrews 11:1 says, "Now faith is the substance of things hoped for, the evidence of things not seen." I couldn't see my vision in the natural, but in the spirit, mentally I did in my mind. Faith is powerful. It is going to be by your faith that you accomplish all your dreams and visions.

I have a great vision in my heart. I think on it constantly and at home, it is written down. I already have the vision of how it is going to be accomplished. With my faith, I believe God that it is going to manifest one day. I don't care how long it may take your vision to come to pass, trust God. He really wants your vision so huge, it's out of your normal thinking. If you yourself can accomplish it in your own strength, this really is not a vision from God. With every great vision, you will need God to bring it to pass. What are you holding in your heart, that's so grand that you are even afraid to speak it out? I was once afraid to speak aloud about my vision. I now speak it out, but only to the right person.

Be careful who you speak your vision to because people you thought were for you, may not be for your vision. Joseph made that mistake in Genesis 37:10-11. He imagined himself being who God had ordained him to be. "Joseph's father rebuked him saying, "What kind of dream is this? Shall I and thy mother, and thy brethren indeed come to bow down ourselves to thee?" His brothers envied him, but his father observed the saying." This is the same today, so you must be careful how you release visions. It is sad but very true. People right in your midst, right in your church will envy the vision God has given you. Sometimes just pardon them in your heart and trust God. Joseph had a dream of his family bowing down to him. Read it in Genesis. Joseph became the commissioner over all the food in the land. Joseph was second to Pharaoh and in power. Yet, his rise to power was for the good of his family. Joseph's family would have perished if he had ignored his vision and walked away. His brothers rose up against him but did not understand what they were doing. Joseph standing over them was not bad; it was good. Even today some people don't understand where God is taking you and your vision. God could raise you up to be a great preacher and use you to help set their family free. We must be careful how we rise up against someone else's vision. Whatever your dream is, write it down and work towards your vision every day. Whatever you do, wait on God and don't rush your vision to come to pass. Trust God and wait on Him. God knows all your plans and visions. "For I know the thoughts that I think toward you, saith the LORD, thoughts of peace, and not of evil, to give you an expected end" (Jeremiah 29:11).

God knows your vision from beginning to the end. He formed you in your mother's womb to do something great in the land. Don't stop dreaming, but stop procrastinating. Don't continue to put your vision and dreams off. You have to get up from where you are and put your hands to your vision. Yes, God will bring the vision to pass. God said in Habakkuk 2:2-3, "Write the vision, and make it plain in tablets, that he who reads it may run. For the vision is yet for an appointed time, but at the end it shall speak, and not lie: though it tarry, wait for it; because it will surely come, it will not tarry." This Scripture explains it all. Wait upon your dream. I do not care how long it has been delayed; wait on it. As I stated before, don't procrastinate. Obey God, write it down, and you must do something; that is run! Run with everything within you. It does not matter if you have to run alone. Imagine you walking in your ordained calling from God. Imagine every dream and vision prospering. It will prosper if you just simply obey God. Imagine this, that you are set free by the power of God walking in victory in every part of your life.

CHAPTER 11

Stand Fast!

Stand fast means to retain your spiritual freedom. Now that you're free, it is going to take wisdom to retain your freedom. Galatians 5:1 says, "Stand fast, therefore, in the liberty wherewith Christ hath made us free, and be not entangled again with the yoke of bondage." When God looses you and fill you with His Spirit, you are free. "Where the spirit of the Lord is, there is liberty" (2 Corinthians 3:17). Liberty is an action going beyond normal limits; it is called freedom! You are free now to serve God and we do this also by serving one another. When we are serving one another in love, we are serving the God in that person. Galatians teaches us how to stand fast, and stay free once you are free. Don't continue to get entangled over and over again. I've seen so many people, once God set them free go back and become entangled again. Often times, this occurs in a manner of a couple of days. There's something wrong when we cannot remain free from one Sunday to the other. What is it causing you to go back in bondage?

Paul said it like this, "It is not I, oh wretched man! It is sin that lies down within." In Romans 7:14-25, Apostle Paul clarifies that the land is spiritual, but he is carnal, sold under sin. For the deeds he does, he does not understand. He goes on to say, "For I don't practice what I should be doing, but instead I do what I hate." Paul admits that if I don't practice what I know the will to be doing, then it is not me, but it is sin within me. He confesses, "It is my flesh, and it is just my carnal mind." There is a war going on! Paul realized that there was no good thing in his flesh, but could not answer why we keep yielding to our flesh? He continued to say, "The good I know I should do; I won't do!" He said, "I found a law, that when I desire to do good, evil is always present."

But this is the thing; if evil is always present, should we yield to evil? The answer is, "Absolutely not!" Paul said, "It is another law working within me, a law warring against the members of my mind, so I don't do the will of the Father." But, he came to a final conclusion. With my mind, I serve the law of God, but with my flesh the law of sin. This is why the mind has to be renewed. The flesh cannot serve God, so if we're walking in our flesh, we're going to fulfill the lust of it. For those who live according to the flesh set their minds on things of the flesh, but those who live according to the Spirit, the things of the Spirit. To be carnally minded is death, but to the spiritually minded is life and peace. The carnal mind is an enemy (hostile) towards God. If we are walking in our flesh, it's impossible to please God. (Romans 8:5-8)

This is why I stated earlier, that we're unable to stand fast from one Sunday to the other. Standing fast or steadfastness takes discipline. I am afraid we as the body of Christ has strayed away from being disciplined. Naturally, we have children so disobedient and so undisciplined, could it be they are attracting these actions from home? To stand fast, you must bring your flesh to a place of discipline. We cannot watch whatever we desire on television. We cannot go everywhere and just drop it. Even as leaders, we have to be very careful to not yield to our flesh for a moment of pleasure. We have to know when to draw the line because the flesh cannot please God. We are losing our victory when we're caught in these sorts of actions. God delivers us out of the yoke of bondage but just to please our flesh, we step right back into that place of bondage. Galatians 5:1 says to not be entangled again. Why did it say again? It is because this happens again, again, and again. It repeats itself over and over again until we recognize the pattern of sin and take a stand against it. This stand is to deal with it at the root; pulling down the stronghold and bringing your flesh under the subjection of God. It is all discipline. We're living in the fast lane world, where the younger and old generations do not know anything about discipline or faithfully practice it. We feel like we can say anything and do anything, and God is please; but He's not. In these current times, the church must set that platform and standard on how to stand fast. Young girls, boys, young men, and women need role models from the church on how to stand fast. Even our young ministers need role models on how to stand fast. It is too much repetitious entanglement in the yoke of bondage occurring. Who will stand in the gap and say, "I choose to live like the bible says?"

Be ye holy for I'm holy (1 Peter 1:16). Temptations are out here, but God will make a way of escape from every temptation; if we will yield to God's spirit and crucify our flesh. Lay down your fleshy desires and God will keep you! Get a made-up mind to be renewed in the members of your mind. Get a made-up mind to yield all your instruments of your body unto God. Get a made-up mind to take on the will of God and not your own will; then you will find yourself walking in the freedom God has for your life. You can stand fast in these last and evil days. You can escape from lustful temptations if you surrender your heart, mind, and soul to God. Jesus is our Savior and He's able to keep us free!

CHAPTER 12

Overcoming Strongholds and Sin Nature

A stronghold is basically like a pattern that has been buried in our minds, causing us to think or receive things in a certain manner. Strongholds hide themselves in the members of your mind. If you allow them to take residence in your mind, strongholds will eventually destroy your life. The fact is that we must get to the root of a stronghold. I look at strongholds as something from Satan, embedded in your heart and mind to hold you in captivity. This is my own definition of a stronghold. When the enemy has planted a lie in your mind, you must pull it down before it destroys your life. For example, the devil tells you God is angry at you for a sin you committed years ago. You ask God to forgive you, but the enemy continues to torment your mind with guilt. This is a manipulation spirit in your mind. It's going to take you getting your mind renewed in order to break free. And do not be conformed to this world but be transformed by the renewing of your mind, so that you may do what the will of God is, that which is good and acceptable, and perfect (Romans 12:2). If you do not renew your mind, you will live a life of condemnation, when God said in His Word in Romans 8 :1 that "there is therefore no condemnation for those who are in Christ Jesus, who walked not according to the flesh but according to the spirit." This clearly lets us know that God does not condemn us. It is Satan who comes in our mind to manipulate and condemn us, with a stronghold that has to be pulled down. God does not hold on our past sinful thoughts and ways. When we became born again, we were cleansed in our hearts, though the residual from our old life remained. This is where we have to confess with our mouths who we are, every time the devil comes to dictate the false perception of who we are in Christ Jesus. The devil is an accuser of the brethren and this is going to be until Jesus returns. The stronghold he plants in our mind can be loosened through the Word of God, if we apply it to our lives. Satan's goal is for the stronghold to hold us in the limited boundaries of condemnation.

Stronghold is defined as a fortified place; a strong man is one who leads or controls by force of will. Let's break the word "stronghold" down. Strong is defined as powerful, violent, not easily broken; not mild or weak. Hold is defined as possessive, restrained, to have a grasp on sustaining to keep in a particular situation. A stronghold will captivate and paralyze you beyond measure. What has you captive to the point you have lost your identity? This is the devil's plan. Demons work behind the scenes of strongholds. The Bible declares that the devil is a liar and he has lied to the members of your mind and painted a false picture of your identity.

Demons are real; however, the church is missing total deliverance. If we are going to break the chains of bondage, we must get to the very root of it. The root is demons working behind the scenes to destroy people. If we tear down the stronghold in a person's life, but don't cast out the demons behind the stronghold, then we have not completed the business of total deliverance. If we are not casting out the demons in that person, then we leave the door open for demons to continue to come and torment the mind of that person. I believe we are counseling demons instead of casting them out! You see, the stronghold is attached to the same uncleaned spirit and we must get to the root and drive it out, so the person is set totally free! I know you are saying to yourself, "This is a deep topic."

It is something rarely talked about in the churches, but it's something that has to be dealt with if we are going to move into the next dimension in God. Strongholds and demons cannot go into the next dimension in God. So, if we do not get delivered, then we are saying we are limited to remain in our own complacent level. There must be deliverance and it must be deliverance now! If the church does not get delivered, then how are we going to get the lost delivered? It has to start with us! I have seen in the last few years, intercessors who are supposed to be already delivered standing around the altar during a deliverance service and not even praying in the spirit. When you know there are intercessors standing there who are supposed to be praying, but they're not delivered themselves, tell me how Satan can cast out Satan? If the prayer warriors are being purged, then what is going to happen with the soul they are supposed to be standing in the gap for? When I have witnessed this in the church, I said, "God, something is wrong if you cannot deliver yourself from strongholds." You cannot get another person delivered from strongholds during deliverance if you're not delivered. You only cause the spirit in them to gain strength. Let's loosed ourselves from strongholds, so we can help others be set free.

CHAPTER 13

Stronglolds and Sin Nature (Part II)

L et's continue our discussion of deliverance in the church from the previous chapter. If we do not get delivered, how are we are going to deliver a lost generation? It starts with us! There is only one Scripture in the New Testament declaring the pulling down of strongholds. 2 Corinthians 10:4: "For the weapons of our warfare are not carnal, but mighty through God to the pulling down of strongholds, casting down imaginations and every high thing that exalts itself against the knowledge of God, bringing every thought into captivity to the obedience of Christ."

I believe we are using the wrong weapons. Our warfare is not of the natural; it's all spiritual. So if we are going to pull down fear, un-forgiveness, strife, lust, pride, and all strongholds that exalt against God, it is going to only be through the spirit of God. Remember the spirit and flesh is at war against one another. Carnally minded is of the flesh and it cannot pull itself down. "Because the carnal mind is enemy against God; for it is not subject to the law of God, neither indeed can be" (Romans 8:7). To begin to deal with strongholds, the mind must be renewed. A lot of these issues start in the mind. This is why God said our weapons are not carnal; our weapons are spiritual, not made of hands. God knew that the only way we were going to conquer the strongholds in our lives and anyone else's life is to conquer it through the spirit and not the flesh. He said to cast down imaginations; vain imaginations, unclean thoughts that come to our minds to remove our focus off the things of God. We must cast these kinds of imagination down! The enemy will always bring vain imaginations to our minds; however, God has given us weapons over those thoughts.

Prayer is a weapon we can use to pull down vain imaginations. We can cry out to God in prayer to purify our thinking. There has to be times of prayer and consecration if you are battling with vain imaginations, and lustful thoughts. This is a chain that will hold you bound from going to the next level in God. Cast down, throw down these hindrances! The Word says to cast down every high thing that exalts itself against God. There are so many things that exalts itself against God; guilt is always exalting itself against God. After God has saved us, guilt always comes to remind us of our past. Therefore, you must cast down this thought. Once God has forgiven us, it is a done deal. Satan is always accusing us of our past and he will be making accusations until Jesus returns. Another stronghold that exalts itself against

God's people is un-forgiveness. If we don't forgive our brethren, how do we expect God to forgive us of our trespasses? I found out un-forgiveness can really block us from the presence of God. There are so many people holding un-forgiveness in the church. We must cast this stronghold down.

I had un-forgiveness against my father for not being there for me and I had to cast it down. God dealt with my heart to forgive and fortunately, I forgave my father before he died. Those chains were tied around my heart tight; however, I was set free by the power of God. I surrendered all to Jesus and the un-forgiveness left my heart. I remember inviting my father to my wedding, even though a part of me just didn't want to do it. Instead, I gave it to God and asked my father to come. I was so happy he came because if he had not, I believe my heart would have been crushed. That was the beginning of my healing when my father accepted my invitation and came to my wedding. Approximately three years later, my father died. I'm so happy I allow God to set me free from un-forgiveness. I could have used my carnal weapon and that was to resent my father or walk in hatred. No, my greatest weapon was love! I loved my father in spite of and healing took place. Our weapons are not carnal, but mighty through God. Love pulled down that stronghold of un-forgiveness, which is one stronghold we must press to always pull down before it overtakes us. It almost took me over! I heard others say that they would not have forgiven their father, so I felt like I had a right to hold un-forgiveness within my heart. We don't have a right to hold un-forgiveness no matter what our parents have or haven't done. Jesus forgave us as we were filthy rags. Yet, He still chose to forgive us. I must admit it is hard to forgive but it is a must! The void in our hearts can be extremely deep and it will feel like a hole is in your soul. But nothing is too hard for God. So, if you're holding that un-forgiveness against a loved one, let it go. You will never get to your destiny with that heavy load. It will weigh you down and slow your pace. God wants you to run into your destiny and you can't until the chains of un-forgiveness are loosed off you!

CHAPTER 14

Strongholds in Sexuality

I s a stronghold in your life? I always say that if anything has a hold on you strongly, you cannot be free in God. I'm about to talk about a stronghold that holds many people in bondage. These are people sitting right in the church committing adultery and fornication. God made sex for a marriage and even though man has made the common-law marriage, it is still a sin. 1 Corinthians 7:2 talks about sexual immorality and instructs us to let every man have his own wife and let every woman have her own husband. Marriage is sacred; therefore, do not be part of the destruction of anyone's marriage. If this is your stronghold, God wants you to break this chain off of your life. Adultery is a sin and sadly, this is going on right in the house of God. It has become so common that those practicing it act as if it is normal.

Frighteningly, it is to the point the persons committing adultery or fornication together believe they will eventually marry each other. Although that may sound insane, they think that it will make it alright, but it doesn't. I have witnessed a pastor out with another woman and I'm looking like this is not the wife I thought he was married to. But that is how fast adultery is happening these days. God is not pleased. Marriage was intended to last until death.

The other stronghold is fornication. Sex outside the bonds of marriage is defined as fornication. We know it happens every day, but does that make it right? Absolutely not! What about the time we spend trying to justify what we are doing wrong in the eyesight of a holy God? When deep in our hearts, we know God is not please. Some use this excuse to live together... "Well, we're getting married soon."

1 Corinthians 6:15-16, says, "Know ye not that your bodies are the members of Christ? Shall I then take the members of Christ and make them the members of a harlot?" God forbid! What? Know ye not that he which is joined to a harlot is one body? for two, saith he, shall be one flesh." Once you have sex with that person, you are joined. This is why God said we sin against our own bodies. Just think about the years you have been fornicating, and add up all those men and women whose spirits are now operating in you.

1 Corinthians 6:18-19 continues the matter of purity. "Flee fornication; every sin that a man doeth is without the body; but he that committed fornication sinneth against his own body. What? Know ye not that your body is the temple of the Holy Ghost which is in you, which ye have of God, and ye are not your

own? For ye are bought with a price: therefore, glorify God in your body, and in your spirit, which are God's."

Our bodies are members of Christ? God is letting us know that when we fornicate, we sin against our own body. The body is sacred, and is the temple of the Lord. In reality, our bodies are not our own. Therefore, we must use our bodies for God's glorification. The chain of fornication is a stronghold and many Christians today struggle with it. It seems to be the norm to "shack" which is the term we used in my day. Today's term is common-law marriage. Nevertheless, it doesn't matter what term is used or how more educated and refined it may sound. It is still called SIN! According to the Word and law of God, sex is for marriage.

Another stronghold is homosexuality and this too has become the norm. However, I believe we as Christians can help a lot of them get set free. We are not here to judge homosexuality, but to shine God's love so brightly it will open their eyes that this kind of lifestyle is not of God. Romans 1:27 says, "And likewise also the men, leaving the natural use of the woman, burned in their lust one toward another; men with men working that which is unseemly, and receiving in themselves that recompence of their error which was meet." God is saying in the Scripture that the male learning the natural use of the female were inflamed in their lusts towards one another; and males with males working shame. The very root of homosexuality is lust! The body lusts for that which is an abomination unto God, but should we judge them? Absolutely not! We must love them just as we do someone who is straight. We love people who fornicate, drink alcohol, and use drugs. Therefore, we must still love homosexuals. It is not them who God hates, but it is the act of the sin He hates. Some homosexuals do not really want to be that way. Some have been hurt so badly by the opposite sex that it caused them to transition to homosexuality. Some have been molested, raped, or just simply betrayed by the opposite sex. Some men turn that way because the spirit entered in through being molested by another male. That spirit entered in and took root and that person began to act out their feelings. They are false feelings the enemy has placed through the act of molestation.

Even through generational curses, I have seen homosexuality follow a family. If you see this trace, then God is allowing you to recognize the trace of sin to take authority over it. Truly, it only takes one born again believer to arrest the generational curse in the spirit realm. Somebody must stand in the gap for their family and curse those actions at the root. God's Word is true and we must stand on it. He said the truth will make us free. Homosexuality is a stronghold and if you are dealing or have dealt in those actions, you can be set free if you desire. There are some who very much love their life of homosexuality and if they don't want to be set free, you cannot set them free. It is only leaving when it, that spirit, is renounced. God said in John 8:36,

"Therefore if the Son sets you free, you shall be free indeed." But, do you want to be free?!

CHAPTER 15

Strongholds in Sexuality (Part II)

As I discussed in Part I of Chapter 14, lust is the root of the strongholds, homosexuality, fornication, adultery, and any sexual sin. If the chains are going to be broken off, then you must realize they will not fall off until you confess that the chains are there and you want to be set free. Lust is a strong man and it is of the flesh. "For the flesh lusted against the spirit and the Spirit against the flesh; and these are contrary the one to the other. So that ye cannot do the things that you would" (Galatians 5:17). Remember, Paul realized he could not do the things that he would do that was right because there was another law working or warring against the law of his mind, bringing him into captivity to the law of sin. Furthermore, Paul understood it really was his flesh warring against his spirit which was drawing him to wrongdoing. I like how Paul identifies the root cause to the war that was going on in his flesh. Flesh and spirit are not on the same level, so there will always be a war between the two.

Naturally so, enemies are always at war. Paul confessed it is sin that lies within. "Therefore do not let sin reign in your mortal body, that you should obey it and its lust" (Romans 6-12). If you allow sin to reign, you are going to obey whoever and whatever is reining. Reign is defined to hold royal office; rule as king. If you allow sin to reign, then you have allowed sin to be king of your body. If allowed, sin will rule your life. The stronghold that has its grasp on you will also rule as king. You will never be free in God as long as sin is reigning in your body.

If you desire truth, you have come to the right place. The Word of God is truth. The truth of the Word of God is that if sin reigns, you are going to obey it in its lust. Allow God to have dominion over your life and not sin. What is that sin, that stronghold you have on the inside that is controlling you? Paul had to identify it in order to be set free. Paul recognized he had no more control over his desires. Each time he tried to do right, sin dictated to him that he was okay. We convince ourselves it is okay, and we know it's a lie from the devil. Confess you have a stronghold and then God can deliver you. Paul confessed. He said "O wretched man am I, who can deliver me from the body of death?" Paul confessed, "If I didn't break free, I'm good as dead".

Romans 6:23 says, "For the wages of sin is death but the gift of God is eternal life through Jesus Christ Our Lord." Many are spiritually dead because sin is reigning in their bodies. There is no way to walk in victory with sin reigning. God is King of kings and Lord of lords. He is the only one reigning. However, when we yield to sin, we become slaves to sin and this brings us into bondage. The sin becomes king over our souls. There is only one king and His name is Jesus.

We have determined that strongholds are controlled by a root called the strongman. "Or else how can we enter into a strong man's house and spoil his goods except he first bind the strongman?" (Matthew 12:29) We must bind up Satan and his demons and God has given us the power to do so. "Verily I say whatsoever ye bind in earth shall be bound in heaven and whatsoever ye shall loose on earth shall be loosed in heaven" (Matthew 18:18). God has already given us the victory over the strongman, the devil, but we must use the keys He has given us. Get to the root of the matter whether it is lust, control, un-forgiveness, anger, rebellion, or whatever that strong man is.

First, recognize and confess it's there. Then you can deal with strongholds and bind it up in Jesus' name. They will not continue to have victory over your life in the name of Jesus. I found out you have to confess strongholds are in your life if you are going to break free from them. There is an authority the people of God have and must walk in. God has already given us power over every spirit that is not like Him. Every spirit is subject to the name of Jesus. This means that every spirit that is not of God is under the subjection and rule of Jesus! If you abide in Jesus, He will abide in you. If the Spirit of God is living in you, then you have power over every unclean spirit. But this only applies if it is in the name of Jesus.

Take your God-given authority and break yourself free with no more chains of strongholds holding you bound! Strongholds are not to have authority over the children of God. We have been equipped to stand against the wiles of the devil. Live your life free from strongholds!

CHAPTER 16

Depression is Real

T his book is entitled *No More Chains*. Why? Because my mission is not to draw people to myself, but it is to draw people to Jesus. There is power in the name of Jesus to break and destroy every chain of bondage. I lived a life for years bound in chains and it is not a good life to live. There were chains of depression, fear, anxiety, confusion, rejection, and abandonment. I can go on and on about life's bondages as I know what it is like to be in bondage, even in life itself. Having dreams and visions, but at the same time feeling inadequate, and just so unqualified to move forward. I know what it feels like to wonder if you will ever have purpose, to live among people who never saw you for who God saw you. Or better yet, people who would see your purpose but would keep it buried or hidden from you, from the fear of you moving ahead of them.

My mission is to set as many as I can from bondage before I leave this earth. This is why I love to write! When this body is too old to preach and cast out devils, I will be doing all I can to write under the inspiration of God. So that through the words on the paper, people will feel the presence of God, and break free from every bondage.

Who told you that you could not be free? In Mark 5:1-8, there was a man bound with chains. The Bible said oftentimes he was in the tomb self-afflicting himself; cutting himself with stones and crying. One day a far off this bound man saw Jesus. He ran up to him, bowed down and worshipped Jesus. He cried with a loud voice, and said, "What must I do with thee, Jesus, thou Son of the Most High God?" You see even demons can recognize the power of Jesus. This is the reason the man bowed down. This man didn't bow down on his own will; the spirit forced him to bow because God declared that every knee shall bow down. Every tongue is going to confess that He is Lord. The demons had to confess who Jesus was!

This man was possessed by many demons and their name was Legion, which meant many. Legion was also the largest unit of the Roman army, consisting between four to six thousand men. Those demons knew Jesus' assignment was to set this man free. This man cried out with a loud voice because he was desperate. When you get desperate you cannot be quiet. You get loud when you really want to be free. The demons asked Jesus to send them into the swine. They knew Jesus had the power to send them out of the man and Jesus granted their request. Jesus didn't send demons to hell because it wasn't judgment time. There will be a time all unclean spirits and demons will be sent to hell to burn in the fire. But Jesus casted them out from tormenting the man. Tormented day and night, this man was desperate and looking for someone to set him free. There was no one in the town walking in the power of Jesus to cast the demons out. But one day, he came face-to-face with the one who could set him free. God is raising up a new generation who may not look like the norm, but down on the inside, they are full of power, the Holy Ghost power to cast the devil out. God is raising up some free folks to free others.

"When thou art converted, strengthen thy brethren" (Luke 22:32). If you are bound, you can't help your brother or sister. There were many around this tormented man who were bound as well. They saw this man everyday cutting himself, crying out in pain; crying out for help, but no one was in position to set the man free. But when he saw Jesus, he took off running. He knew there was the Son of the living God, who could wash away his sins and set him free. Jesus didn't waste any time and commanded the demons to let the man go. Later the people in the city saw the man sitting; he was clothed and in his right mind. As long as this man was tormented by the devil, he could not fulfill his purpose. Tied with chains, people are walking around bound, and the enemy knows they cannot fulfill their purpose. Jesus loosed the chains off the man, and He wants to do the same thing for you.

Chains of guilt, shame, regret, rejection, depression, oppression, fear, doubt, and every binding spirit had me chained down. It took quite a while for me to be set free, and honestly every day, I am still breaking free. Some may ask why you're breaking free? Why you don't just say break free? Every day of your life something will try to tie you up. Therefore, I say, *breaking*, because it is a continuous process that occurs daily. When you become free from one thing, here comes the devil trying to bind you up. Thus, constantly I'm breaking free!

Layers of hurt, and shame can take years for you to finally break! I am free, but still breaking free. You may say that doesn't make any sense. How is that possible? I will explain it like this. I broke free from lust of the flesh, pride of life, and lust of the eyes. I believe God broke me free totally. There is no temptation there and I have learned how to live a daily life free from lust of the flesh, and lust of the eyes. Now the pride of life, I must say comes to tempt me. I can still feel God breaking pride from my life. Each day in our lives, we have to go through the process of breaking from spirits. There was a time depression was a stronghold in my life. I spent days depressed and sometimes I didn't even know I was depressed. It had become such the norm, that I didn't realize I was living a fake life. In church, I would put on the fake face like everything was going well. I looked nice from the outside. I was dressed to kill, but my heart was aching from many disappointments. There was so much hurt from feeling abandoned as a child. So much hurt from feeling rejected by your first love. So much pain in my soul that I thought I couldn't live anymore. I was only 18 years old and my heart was crushed. The young man I thought I would spend my life with after dating throughout high school crushed my heart. I felt as though I couldn't trust ever again. Even after meeting and marrying the true love God had for me, I walked around still hurting. The man God sent to me is Michael Teele, my husband of almost 30 years now. This man was used by God to start the chains falling off. Michael was able to reach where nobody else could and I knew I would spend the rest of my life with him. If you are depressed and single, it is important you connect with someone who can help you find yourself. Someone who God can use to help you break free. I once was bound but now I am free; no more chains holding me!

CHAPTER 17

Go, Stand and Speak!

One day I grasped that I could not go, stand and speak until God loosed the chains! This is what the Lord told the Apostles in Acts 5:19. Peter and the other apostles were healing the sick, and signs and wonders were performed among the people. People would become healed by the shadow of Peter! The apostles were doing a great work for God and people with evil spirits were getting delivered. The Bible says that another group of people were there too; the high priests and Sadducees. They were religious, but had no relationship with God. These people rose up against the apostles for doing a great work for God. I am a witness as it has happened to me. My heart's desire is only to love and please God as I choose to obey God rather than man. I have seen jealousy and strife rise up against me for no reason. I cried many nights to the point of bringing myself into bondage. I was so bound with chains of oppression, guilt, and shame. I would ask God what had I done? God began to let me see that it was just jealousy and strife. I even asked God if I was worshipping Him from a bad spirit. I had chains of self-blame and would always try to find fault in my own self. I had allowed people's jealousy of me operating in the anointing to bring me under bondage. I would go home, beating myself up; sometimes feeling like I wasn't good enough for God. People can make you feel so low sometimes. But once I broke free from people's opinion about myself, then I was able to go, stand, and speak what God had anointed me to do.

So many are spiritually tied with chains of bondage; therefore, they cannot complete their mission from God. Peter and the other apostles were thrown into prison from preaching and laying hands on people, who were healed. The angel of the Lord appeared at the prison and opened the prison doors and brought them out. The angel of the Lord told them to go, stand, and speak in the temple the words God had given them. The apostles and Peter didn't waste any time. The next day, they were out fulfilling their mission from God. I remember being bound and disobedient to what I was called to do. I allowed fear and condemnation from man to hinder me from my mission. Nevertheless, one day, God freed me from the spirit of bondage, and I've been running ever since!

If you know there is a specific mission God has appointed you to complete, don't stop until the mission is completed. Suppose Peter and the apostles had allowed the Sadducees to stop them? Many people would have never been healed and set free. Think about people who God has planned to be in your path, to be healed or delivered from your anointing. If you allow people to put chains on you or throw you into a spiritual prison, then you're hindering yourself from being free, and so many others are depending on you! As I said earlier, Peter and the apostles didn't waste time after God loosed them from the prison. They went right back out praying, preaching, and teaching the Gospel of Jesus Christ. We must do the same. Once God sets us free, remember our freedom is for someone else. I can tell you today I'm free and feel wonderful. I know what it feels like to shut completely down because of people. I remember being depressed because I was rejected. When you're rejected by the world or the streets, it hurts. But it really hurts when you're rejected by your own sisters and brothers in Christ. John 1:11 says, "He (Jesus) came unto his own, and his own received him not." Rejection can crush your heart, but God is a healer of our hearts.

To you today who has a call on your life, and your own will not receive you, according to God's Word, you must shake the dust from your feet and move on (Matthew 10:14). Will you not answer the call because people put chains on you? No! But do as Peter and the apostles did. Go, stand, and speak what God has put in your mouth! The Bible said Peter said to the Sadducees, should we "ought to obey God rather than men?" You must obey God rather than men. You may suffer and face many trials, but stand still and see the salvation of the Lord. There are too many souls at stake to disobey God to please man. Be a God pleaser and not a man pleaser. Go, stand, and speak! Obey God and be free! No more chains!

CHAPTER 18

No More Chains...
Bondage Free!

I am determined in my heart and mind that there will be no more chains in my life! I am living my life every day with *No More Chains*. I can't teach you how to *Break Free*, if I am bound with chains. I want to be totally free to help set the captives free. Bondage is a terrible state or condition as Webster's dictionary describes it as slavery, one who has lost his liberty and has no rights. We that have been set free are called to set the captives free. However, if the preachers are not free ourselves, how can we help others? Romans 2:21-22 says, "Thou therefore which teachest another, teaches thou not thyself? thou that preachest a man should not steal, dost thou steal? thou that sayest a man should not commit adultery, dost thou commit adultery? thou that abhorrest idols, dost thou commit sacrilege?" This passage of Scripture is basically asking simple questions. If you're not free, then how do you preach it? Don't be preaching others to break free if you're bound in chains. I've done that a lot in the past, but praise Jesus I am finally free! I can preach freedom in to the fullest. I know that there's no more chains holding me. I had to experience living in bondage and breaking free from bondages, to preach the acceptable year of the Lord. We should want our lives to reflect what we preach, unless we be a cast away. We should be a guide to the blind, and a light to them who are in darkness.

I'm telling you bondage is a dark place to live in. Just take a moment and think about a person in a dark, cold, lonely jail cell. It's not a happy place to be. It's a place of confinement and darkness, absolutely no liberty. This is why my heart is so compassionate about ministering to the bound. My desire is to see you free because this is what God did for me. Once the Son set you free you shall be free indeed! Once God frees you, this will be your life's testimony as I have allowed my freedom to be my testimony. As loud as I can and every chance I can, I am shouting, "There is a Savior! His name is Jesus, who will set you free if you want to be free."

You can live a lifestyle of freedom every day of your life. There is a peace like never released in your life once God frees you. In reality, we are already free but we just have to receive it. Definitely, no born again believer should be walking around bound.

Therefore, we are buried with him by baptism into death: that like as Christ was raised up from the dead by the glory of the Father, so we also should walk in the newness of life. For if we

have been planted in the likeness of His death, we shall be also in the likeness of His resurrection; knowing this, that our old man is crucified with Him, that the body of sin might be destroyed, that henceforth we should not serve sin. For he that is dead is freed from sin.
(Romans 6:4-7)

If we have been resurrected through the shed blood of Jesus, we are free. Once we die in God, we are resurrected (freed) through the death of Jesus, but we too must die to ourselves; die to the old man. Our old man is our flesh which Jesus has already freed us from. It was *No More Chains* when our Savior hung on that cross and said, "It is finished!" In other words, He was saying *No More Chains*; the Son has set you free! We have to receive this freedom and live it out, because it's already done! Look back at the Scripture. It says, "If we have been planted together in the likeness of His death." Notice it says "likeness" of His death. Our flesh (the old man) dies in the likeness of Jesus dying for our sins. It's our flesh being crucified in the likeness of His crucifixion. It is our will, our old ways, and old man crucified as Jesus was crucified. Then we are resurrected in the newness of life with a new spirit! *No More Chains*! We are no longer bound to sin! We will serve Jesus, not sin. Therefore, we are no longer entangled in the yoke of bondage. For whoever is dead to sin is free indeed!

Man can free you one day, turn around the next day and bring you back into bondage. NOT Jesus! He is the same today, yesterday and tomorrow! Yield to God and be set free today!

Romans 6:16 says, "Know ye not that whom ye yield yourselves servants to obey, his servants ye are to whom ye obey; whether of sin unto death, or of obedience unto righteousness?" We are slaves to whatever or whomsoever we obey. If you are willfully in sin, then you're not free. Either you're going to serve God or sin. Which will you choose? Choose today which you will serve.

Roman's 6:18 says, "Being then made free from sin, ye became the servants of righteousness." Once we're freed from sin, then we are servants of God. If you're living in adultery, you're bound and serving adultery, not Jesus. That sin holds you bound, and you're unable to serve God wholeheartedly. Instead of serving God, you're serving your old man (your flesh). Romans 8:2 reveals for the law of the Spirit of life in Jesus hath made us "FREE" from the law of sin and death. Accepting Jesus as your Lord and Savior, believing that He died, rose, and His death conquered sin and death, is our Freedom! *No More Chains*!

I pray that this book *No More Chains* will help the lost as well as those who are saved, but living a lie. You think you're free but chains are holding you bound. I pray that you will share your testimony how once God freed you, and now you're free indeed! Let someone know that they can be set free by the power of Jesus. We're no longer bound; we're free. *No More Chains* holding me!

My Prayer for You

Warfare Prayer to Break Bondages

Father God who is the only true God, You are the beginning and the end. You reign above every situation in our lives. Heavenly Father, you are King of kings and Lord of lords; besides you there is none other. Thank You for being ruler over every spirit of darkness. Thank You that You have given me authority over all depressions, addictions, and every unclean spirit. You told us to put on the whole armor of God, that we can stand against the darkness of the world. For we wrestle not against flesh and blood, but against principalities, against powers, against the rulers of darkness. Father, now in the name of Jesus, I bind up every principality that's warring against my mind, body, and spirit, and every unclean spirit coming against the very will of God for my life. Spiritual wickedness warring against my family, I bind in the name of Jesus for no weapon formed against me and my family shall prosper. In the name of Jesus, I pull down every stronghold that's trying to hold me in bondage, and I loose my mind and spirit to serve You for I am not a slave to the spirit of darkness in the name of Jesus. I pull down darkness, and every evil work warring against my thoughts, the will of God, my body, and my spirit. Father, You said the weapons of my warfare are not carnal but mighty through God in the pulling down of every stronghold. You have given me the power in Jesus' name to bring it under the captivity of God. I now break the spirit of lack off of my life and my family's life. Above all things, you wish that we will prosper and be in health. In Your Word, You said You're able to do exceedingly abundantly above all I can ask or think, according to the power that works in me in Jesus' name. Peace be loosed upon my mind, strength be loosed, and the gates of hell be bound forever! I shall walk in victory, for I am the righteousness of Jesus Christ, not by might nor by power but by the spirit of the God. Lord, I reign with You, so I thank You for the victory, the peace, and deliverance that's already done in my life. In Jesus' name, I pray! May Your presence always abide in me as I abide in You! Amen!

Keys to Loose
and
Keys to Bind

Matthew 18:18

Verily I say unto you, Whatsoever ye shall bind on earth shall be bound in heaven: and whatsoever ye shall loose on earth shall be loosed in heaven.

Matthew 16: 18 - 19

And I say also unto thee, That thou art Peter, and upon this rock I will build my church; and the gates of hell shall not prevail against it. 19 And I will give unto thee the keys of the kingdom of heaven: and whatsoever thou shalt bind on earth shall be bound in heaven: and whatsoever thou shalt loose on earth shall be loosed in heaven.

Seven Keys...

1. Pray without ceasing.
2. Read and study the Word of God.
3. Have days of Fasting.
4. Have a day of quiet and meditation on God.
5. Keep positive company
6. Surround yourself with people who speak truth into you.
7. Stay connected to a ministry that preaches the grace of God, not bondage!

Seven Days of Fasting and Prayer
(To Usher You into God's Presence)

Day One

What is Fasting?

Fasting – biblical term for going without food. The noun translated "fast" or "a fasting" is its own in the Hebrew and Nigeria in the Greek. It means voluntary abstinence from food. The literal Hebrew translation would be "not to eat."

This morning as you rise, take time to pray and meditate before God. Ask His guidance on how you fast according to your work place or business. Everyone is different and so I always direct people to ask God to lead and guide them mainly how to fast. It's between you and God!

Matthew 6: 16 - 18. *Moreover, when ye fast, be not, as the hypocrites, of a sad countenance; for they disfigure their faces that they may appear unto men to fast. Verily I say unto you, they have their reward. But thou, when thou fastest, anoint thine head, and wash their face; that thou appear not unto men to fast, but unto thy Father which is in secret: and thy Father, which seeth in secret, shall reward thee openly.*

Note: God is not impressed with our fasting, so never fast to impress God or men. Our fast should be for the right motive. Our reasoning for fasting should be like Isaiah 58 says. It should be and for only to loose the bands of wickedness, to undo the heavy burden and to let the oppressed go free.

Notes for Day One

Write down your first day experience, and some things you're expecting to see spiritually in your seven-day journey of fasting and praying.

_____

_____

_____

_____

_____

_____

_____

_____

_____

_____

_____

_____

_____

_____

_____

_____

_____

_____

Notes for Day One

Notes for Day One

_____

_____

_____

_____

_____

_____

_____

_____

_____

_____

_____

_____

_____

_____

_____

_____

_____

_____

_____

_____

_____

Notes for Day One

_____

_____

_____

_____

_____

_____

_____

_____

_____

_____

_____

_____

_____

_____

_____

_____

_____

_____

_____

_____

_____

Day Two

Fasting and Praying

Mark 9:29. *And he said unto them, this kind can come forth by nothing, but by prayer and fasting.*

In the book of Mark, a person who had a child foaming from the mouth, possessed with a dumb spirit, brought his child to the disciples to cast the spirit from the child, but he said the disciples couldn't cast the demon out. Jesus said, "O faithless generation, how long shall I be with you? How long shall I suffer you? Bring him unto me (Mark 9:19). Jesus was saying to His disciples, "Haven't you learned anything? Don't you know by now that this kind of spirit requires you to be in prayer and fasting?"

This generation just does not believe it's going to take fasting and a lifestyle of prayer for what we're facing in the last days. Satan can't cast out Satan. If you're indulging in sinful activities and not consecrating yourself before God, these kinds of spirits are not coming out. Even in us at times, there are spirits. Yes, you can be saved and still have spirits attack you. Therefore, we must fast and pray. No longer can we just go through the motions of church antics. From the passage of Scripture, we can gather that the disciples didn't equip themselves. Jesus fed them and gave them good instructions and teachings, but did they take heed?

Evidently not! Or they could have cast out the spirit from the child. We must fast and pray.

Notes for Day Two

Take notes today from the Scriptures provided for Day Two. Write down some experiences you have faced, and you knew you weren't equipped to pray for someone else. Take this lesson in and decide you will take heed to the Word of God.

_____

_____

_____

_____

_____

_____

_____

_____

_____

_____

_____

_____

_____

_____

_____

_____

Notes for Day Two

_____

_____

_____

_____

_____

_____

_____

_____

_____

_____

_____

_____

_____

_____

_____

_____

_____

_____

_____

_____

_____

_____

_____

_____

_____

_____

Notes for Day Two

Notes for Day Two

Day Three

Declare a Fast Ordained by God

Esther 4:16. *Go, gather together all the Jews that are present in Shushan, and fast ye for me, and neither eat nor drink three days, night or day; I also and my maidens will fast likewise; and so, will I go in unto the King, which is not according to the law: and if, I perish, I perish.*

Here we have Esther declaring a fast amongst the people to save her entire generation. Mordecai got the word to Esther; that Haman the enemy of Mordecai had plotted to have all the Jews destroyed. This was an enemy against the Jews and Esther knew the only way to destroy this devil was by fasting and praying. Remember the Bible says these kinds come out only by fasting and prayer. Esther knew this would be a significant risk, but she knew she had to go see the king to save her generation. Esther was wise; she told Mordecai to go gather all the Jews that were in Shushan, and fast for her, to neither eat nor drink for three days and nights. She knew she needed some people standing in the gap before she went before the king. Esther risked her life for a generation; in those days if you went before the king without an invitation, you would be killed. Yet, Esther declared, "If I perish, let me perish!" She went and God showed her favor and saved a whole generation, because she declared a fast. Will you declare a fast for your family and save a generation?

Notes for Day Three

Today write down your family members and other families you know who are under attack from the enemy. Bring some praying family members together and declare a fast on behalf of your family.

_____

_____

_____

_____

_____

_____

_____

_____

_____

_____

_____

_____

_____

_____

Notes for Day Three

Notes for Day Three

Day Four

Great Will Be Your Reward!

Matthew 6:18. *That thou appear not unto men to fast, but unto thy Father which is in secret; and thy Father, which seeth in secret, shall reward thee openly.*

When you gather together the family members you listed on Day Three's Notes to fast, do not announce or discuss this with others. Our fast should be unto God. Gather a few praying partners who will pray in secret, be sincere and not gossip. It's time to get serious with our praying and fasting. I have never seen so many Christians and preachers too with no prayer life. Jesus prayed to the Father, so that's foolish to think we don't suppose to have a prayer life. Some say it doesn't take all of this, but it really does! The world is filled with chaos and confusion. Families are going through and churches are facing wicked principalities and wickedness in high places. There is no doubt in my mind and heart that we all need prayer. No one is exempt, from the poorest person to the wealthiest person; we all need it. Fasting and praying isn't something you broadcast; but God will reward us openly when we fast and pray in secret. Let's look at Moses' example of how God rewarded him openly before the children of Israel in Exodus 33 - 34. Moses spent time in God's presence and the glory was shining on him publicly! When you fast, and pray, people will see the glory on your life and will see God moving

113

openly on your circumstances. Just fast and pray; be quiet and let God do the talking by rewarding you openly.

Notes for Day Four

List the things you want God to do personally for you that you haven't discussed with anyone. Let this day be very intimate and sacred between you and God. Write down your secrets and confessions to God. He will reward you openly!

_____

_____

_____

_____

_____

_____

_____

_____

_____

_____

_____

_____

_____

_____

_____

Notes for Day Four

Notes for Day Four

Notes for Day Four

_____

_____

_____

_____

_____

_____

_____

_____

_____

_____

_____

_____

_____

_____

_____

_____

_____

_____

_____

_____

_____

_____

_____

Day Five

Ordained by God or Man?

Acts 14:23. *And when they had ordained them elders in every church, and had prayed with fasting, they commended him to the Lord, on whom they believed.*

This Scripture is mainly for pastors and bishops, who ordain ministers for the working of the ministry. It is important that pastors fast and pray before ordaining people. The Bible says to not lay hands suddenly on no man. Why are we so quick to send people out unequipped? I believe one reason is we're building membership this way. I'm skeptical when I attend service at a small church and out of 25 members, 15 of them are ministers. Everybody has not been chosen by God. It's important for leaders to lay before God and consult Him before ordaining ministers and taking matters into their own hands. People are making a mess out here now because they have been ordained by man and not God. God is not pleased with these actions. I see people getting ordained who are committing adultery or fornication. Their character is so far from the title they are holding in the church. Therefore, God is calling us to fast and pray to receive the needed direction and instructions in our lives. I would rather just sit in the back of the church until I learn what is truth, than to be pulled up to receive a title, knowing I'm not in right standards with God.

Leaders, please fast and pray before ordaining and handing out titles.

Notes for Day Five

If you are a pastor, write down some mistakes you have made in ordaining or placing people in positions without fasting and praying. Be honest with yourself and God; then ask Him if this is one of the reasons your church is not growing. If you are not, then write down when you knew you were not in right standards with God and you took on a title/position unworthily. What did you learn or will do differently now?

_____

_____

_____

_____

_____

_____

_____

_____

_____

_____

_____

Notes for Day Five

Notes for Day Five

Notes for Day Five

Day Six

Choose the Fast of God

Isaiah 58:6. *Is not this the fast that I have chosen? To loose the bands of wickedness, to undo the heavy burdens, and to let the oppressed go free, and that ye break every yoke?*

God was letting us know He must call the fast for it to be effective and ordained by God. A lot of fasts we're doing are of man and we're seeing no results. If God didn't call it, then you might as well EAT! God said in the Scripture we read that His fast breaks every yoke and loose the bands of wickedness. The fast of God breaks every chain in our lives. It will set the captive free and deliver us from lust. But because we are not listening to God and doing our own thing, we are not experiencing deliverance in our churches and our homes. We need to ask ourselves whether we are just dieting or fasting. Remember that this is what got Eve and Adam in trouble. Satan tempted them with food, a piece of fruit. Then he tried to tempt Jesus with food, while He was fasting in the wilderness. The devil told Jesus to turn the stone into bread. This is clear evidence that the devil never wants us to fast and pray because even he knows the benefits. He knows that when we get serious about praying and fasting, we're going to tear his dark kingdom down! Check your motive when you fast. Make sure it's the fast to break yokes and loose the bands of wickedness; not for selfish gain.

125

Notes for Day Six

Today ask yourself, "Why am I really doing this seven-day fast?" Before you start it, make sure you have the right motive. Name some strongholds you want loosed out of your life or family members' lives.

_____

_____

_____

_____

_____

_____

_____

_____

_____

_____

_____

_____

_____

_____

_____

Notes for Day Six

_____

_____

_____

_____

_____

_____

_____

_____

_____

_____

_____

_____

_____

_____

_____

_____

_____

_____

_____

_____

_____

_____

_____

Notes for Day Six

Day Seven

Follow the Example of Jesus

The spirit indeed is willing; but the flesh is weak.
(Matthew 26:41)

Today, I want you to meditate on the very importance of *why* you're fasting. I know this is the last day, but as you end it, think about our Savior Jesus Christ. In this Scripture, we are reminded how our spirit is willing to do right, but the flesh is not; therefore, we must fast and pray. Jesus was in the garden of Gethsemane, and He asked the disciples to pray for Him. But when He returned from praying, they were asleep. They were willing to pray with Jesus for one hour, but their flesh couldn't withstand it, because of its weakness. Therefore, the flesh must come under subjection of the Spirit of the Lord. Fasting and prayer brings the flesh under the authority of the Spirit of God! Remember Jesus fasted 40 days and 40 nights; and afterward the devil came and tempted Him. Jesus overcame the temptations of Satan, through fasting and prayer, so we likewise must do the same. If you are a Christian and you're not taking the time to fast and pray, I can assure you that many decisions you make in this life will be from your emotions and intellect, but not your spirit. Allow God to lead you as you fast and pray, but He cannot lead you if you refuse to submit to His will. You will learn to submit to God's will, as you learn how to fast and pray. If Jesus did, who are we to say that we can't?

Notes for Day Seven

Write down notes on your temptation experiences. Then name some victories in your life that you know you have overcome because of fasting and prayer.

_____

_____

_____

_____

_____

_____

_____

_____

_____

_____

_____

_____

_____

_____

_____

_____

_____

Notes for Day Seven

Notes for Day Seven

Notes for Day Seven

Meet the Author

Evangelist Latina Teele is a native of Greenville, North Carolina. She has been married to her husband Michael Teele for 30 years and through this union, they have three children, Michael, Latilya, and Jeremiah and one goddaughter Mimi. Latina joined the body of Christ through salvation in 1990 under the leadership of Pastor Brady Carmack of Popular Point Missionary Baptist Church. Latina later joined her husband Michael Teele at the House of Refuge Church in 1997 under the leadership of Pastor Ronnie Staton.

In 2001, Latina preached her initial sermon with a powerful message to the body of Christ titled "Be Loosed to Be Used." In 2006 she was ordained as an Elder of the church. For years, Latina spread the gospel of Christ by traveling throughout eastern NC and surrounding areas.

Latina released her first gospel CD in 2002 titled, "Be Loosed to Be Used." In 2005, she released her second CD titled "It's Already Done." Later, in 2008 she released her third CD titled "A Fool for You." Latina has a worshipper's heart and love spreading the Word of God through the gift of music.

In 2012, Latina published her first book, *Be Loosed to Be Used.* This book talks about the tied donkey loosed to be used by God in Matthew 21:7. In 2014, Latina published her second book *Breaking Free,* which is the second part to *Be Loosed to Be Used.* Then, in 2016, Latina released her third book *Worship at The Well,* a 21-day devotional that teaches you how to worship God and to never thirst again. Lastly, in 2017, the book *Living Every Day in God's Presence* was birthed.

She is the founder of Oasis Learning Center and Oasis Evangelistic Outreach where she spreads and sings the Gospel of Jesus Christ. Evangelist Teele is also the founder of Breaking Free Ministries, which aired on The Now Network from 2018-1019. Now, Evangelist Teele airs her weekly broadcast on her social media platform.

Contact Information for Evangelist Latina Teele:

Website: www.latinateele.com

Email Address: latinateele@gmail.com

Facebook: @LartinaTeeleMinistries

Made in the USA
Middletown, DE
11 April 2023

27768306R00076